Published by:

The Learning Net

Lake City, FL

Copyright © 2014

Library of Congress Cataloging-in-Publication Data

Perry, William G., 1947 -

   Code / William G. Perry

ISBN-13: 978-1477660287
ISBN-10: 1477660283

Publications by the Learning Net are available to booksellers and distributors world-wide. Microsoft and Windows are either registered trademarks or trademarks of Microsoft Corporation in the United States and/or other countries. Other product and company names mentioned herein may be the trademarks of their respective owners.

Printed by: The Learning Net

     Lake City, FL

Introduction

Computers have completely changed the way we live and work.

People have embraced digital processing technology and the Internet at a faster rate than they accepted television. Many homes and most businesses own and operate more than one computer. Mobile computing supported by smart phones and tablets is expanding rapidly.

We frequently visit Facebook to keep up with our friends, Twitter to "tweet" and YouTube for the latest hot video clip. Our electronic devices seem to do it all. We send and receive huge volumes of e-mail and texts, balance our checkbooks and buy what we need – all from our desktop computers, tablets and smart phones.

Small businesses routinely store their most important information on computers and depend upon critical customer records to be available at the click of a mouse or the tap of a screen.

But there is a dark side to our ability to connect.

We live in an intense threat environment. Our digital information and everything that goes with it are at serious risk. Multiple threats stalk the Internet looking for computers with vulnerabilities to exploit. There are thousands of active threats. As soon as one "fix" or patch is written to plug a security hole others arise.

How did we get into such a bind? The answer is simple. The Internet was purposely designed to be "open". Very little thought was given to security when the Internet was first invented. I know, I was there.

The creators of the Internet were unaware of how it would be used in the future. Only a small number of computers were being used in the decade of the 60's. Networks and consumer devices, as we know them today, didn't exist.

The need to protect credit card numbers, trade secrets, bank accounts and social security numbers was of little concern when the Internet was invented. This fact has tremendous implications for us today.

Because the Internet is so vulnerable, we have little choice but to actively protect our information assets. We are, otherwise, guaranteed to become victims of hackers and cyber criminals if we fail to do so.

The original purpose of the Internet was to easily share information among remote computers in the event of a national emergency. Only the military, scientists in laboratories and universities had access to the Internet in the beginning. The Web and e-commerce were nearly thirty years away from becoming a reality.

Here's our reality today: We are dependent upon an information system developed in the 1960's that was designed to make connecting to other computers easy.

Unless you follow a robust security plan with your computers you are living with an "unlocked front door," "open windows" and "unattended cash drawers". It's just that simple.

You have to become actively involved in securing your digital assets.

The purpose of this book is to help you understand what you need to do to protect your information infrastructure against the threat environment in which you function.

"Please visit www.computer-security-glossary.org for definition of computer security terms and related articles".

Chapter 1

What Dangers Do Your Computers Face?

Your computer operates in an incredibly dangerous threat environment. You must take steps to limit the risks, threats and vulnerabilities.

What are Risks, Threats and Vulnerabilities?

A "risk" against your digital assets becomes a reality when a hacker unleashes a "threat" on the Internet and finds a "vulnerability" on your computer or device (i.e. tablet or smart phone).

An example of a "threat" would be a gang of international cyber thieves seeking to steal credit card account numbers. A "vulnerability" would be the absence of anti-virus software on your computer to prevent unauthorized entry.

The bad guys are continuously on the Internet scanning computers that are in use around the world looking for those that have vulnerabilities. One specific technique used by cyber thieves or hackers is known as "port scanning."

When an unprotected "port" or open door on a computer system is discovered, the "vulnerability" can be exploited. Malicious software can be installed on your computer and hackers can gain control of your system.

You may be unaware that there are more than 65,000 "ports" associated with connecting your computer to the Internet. Each of these connections seeks to access or respond to another computer on the Internet unless the user secures the ports to make them unavailable.

Threats to home and small business computer systems, today, remain strong. The latest Computer Crime and Security Survey reports that malware (software designed to invade and take control of your computer) remains the largest single attack method. The same survey reports that nearly half of all of the respondents experienced some type of attack against their computers.

We are losing ground in the cyber security battle. The types of attacks keep changing. The nature of the malware is becoming more sophisticated. The advantage now belongs to the attacker. On top of more complicated attacks, the growth in the number of *end points* (i.e. tablets, iPhones, etc.) contributes to the problem.

The huge growth in mobile computing devices has only expanded the number of risks against confidential information.

The crime survey reference reported financial losses that averaged $100,000 per respondent and went up to as high as $25,000,000. Slightly less than one-half of the respondents (45.6%) reported having experienced a *targeted* attack. That means the bad guys went after a particular computer on purpose.

More than one-third of the individuals (38.9%) who reported information on the survey had been the victim of phishing scams. (See www. computer-security-glossary.org for the definition.)

The study candidly admits that most people (and businesses in particular) avoid reporting security breaches to the law enforcement officials.

The report stated: *"There is much more illegal and unauthorized activity going on in cyberspace than corporations admit to their clients, stockholders and business partners or report to law enforcement. Incidents are widespread, costly and commonplace."* - **Crime Security Institute Director.**

The same would be true with ordinary individuals. The truth is that we would have great difficulty in knowing how many personal computers have experienced an attack. Most law enforcement agencies will file a report of a cyber crime, but in most cases your local police are without the means to conduct an investigation and apprehend the criminal.

The victims of cyber crime are essentially left to fend for themselves.

But why would anyone be interested in breaking into my computer?

Many computer users fail to understand why breaking into their home and small business computers would be of any value.

The reasons that malicious attackers want to attack your home or business computer systems are varied. Some are teen-aged hackers breaking into computers "just to have fun". Other more nefarious intruders are out to steal your credit card numbers, those of your customers, your identity or to hijack your computing resources and steal proprietary information.

Let's be clear. The widespread and growing use of the Internet raises the probability that risks may be realized. Many Internet connections are persistent (always on) and, unless protected, increase the ways in which vulnerabilities can be exploited.

Hackers wanting to break into your computer might only be interested in gaining access to your resources to <u>mask</u> an attack on other computers. These crackers want to steal privately owned memory or bandwidth and use it for their own purposes.

Nefarious users who gain control of your information system can use it to conduct illegal activities, such as launching attacks against other systems that might be "juicier targets." By masquerading as <u>you</u>, to distribute his/her attack, the identity of the bad guy can be more easily cloaked. One bad guy can enroll thousands of computers to attack the information infrastructure of others. Your computer can become part of a "bot army" or might even be used in illegal drug or human trafficking.

Your computer could be infected with "keyboard loggers". They are capable of capturing your key strokes, and providing access to your private information. Crackers might also be interested in your password at work. Malware is capable of storing your sensitive information and sending it to the intruder at a time of his or her own choosing.

The people who break into your home or small business computer might be interested in obtaining your bank account number and stealing your money or in downloading proprietary or sensitive personal information.

Home and small business computer systems tend to be dreadfully unprotected and highly vulnerable.

The following story happened to a member of the author's family.

A relative purchased educational software for his family at a national retail store chain. A major toy manufacturer in the United States had created the computer software, unbeknownst to the family, designed to install on the family's home computer.

Shortly after installing the software the father discovered that the computer was "dialing-out" and connecting to the publisher's remote site. The children's activities had apparently been collected and uploaded to the manufacturer's computer. That is frightening.

The parent, rightfully so, felt that information collected on his children was private and that the manufacturer's unauthorized use of his computing resources represented outright theft.

What Else Can Happen?

We've shown that a malicious hacker can gain access to your computer and collect information about your private financial records and work-place secrets. There is an endless list of information that unauthorized intruders can access if they have control of your computer.

Among the very real dangers facing your computer is a list shown below:

- Loss of important personal information (i.e. tax records, pictures, health care related information, etc.)
- Loss of your digital identity
- Endangerment of your family members
- Loss of privacy
- Financial losses
- Damage to your computer
- Hardware and software failures
- Loss of vital customer records if you run a small business.

Your identity can be sold on the open market or your company's sensitive information can be sent to a key competitor. Your personal family calendar, for example, can be downloaded to determine when your home will be vacant. Heaven forbid that information gleaned from your computer can help a criminal stalk you or a family member.

Summary

Theft of information from your home or small business computer has become one of the fastest growing crimes. It's clearly a low-risk, high reward crime for the criminal. A majority of the time the identity of the attacker isn't even known.

You should be aware of the types of risks that can be realized and become proactive in stopping cyber criminals. We'll look next at what you can do to protect your information assets.

You'll need to assess the threats and vulnerabilities that you are up against.

Chapter 2

How Vulnerable is Your Computer?

Can you answer the following questions?: *1.) Do you know how vulnerable your computer is to existing threats? 2.) Do you know what information you cannot afford to lose? 3.) Do you have an information security plan?*

You have a major information security problem if you answer "No" to the above questions or you aren't sure.

The safest approach for small business and home computer users is to assume that **ALL** of the information on your computer is critical and must be made secure. Large companies can finance the isolation of critical information resources based upon software and hardware engineering. You don't have the resources to do so if you are like most people. So, what can you do?

One thing you can do as an individual or small business owner is to assess your own vulnerabilities.

You can determine the vulnerability of your computer system by performing what is known as a "white hat hack" on your own computer.

Perform a White Hat Hack on Your System

Either you or a third party can perform the same type of scanning or probing of your system that malicious users would do to determine if your system has vulnerabilities that can be exploited. One of the third-party companies that performs this service is Gibson Research.

You are encouraged to test the vulnerability of your system now. Use the Internet to access Gibson Research (www.grc.com) and run their **"Shields UP"** series of tests. Doing so is **FREE**. The experience can be eye-opening.

When you arrive at the Gibson Research website, look for the words "**Shields UP**" which you can find scrolling down to the topic, 'Hot Spots'. Click on the "**Shields UP**" link and follow the instructions.

Gibson Research must have your permission to run the "white hat hack" on your system. When you "click" on the "**Shields Up**" link you'll see text similar to that which follows. You need to read it.

Please take just a moment to read and consider these three points:

Your use of the Internet security vulnerability profiling services on this site constitutes your FORMAL PERMISSION for us to conduct these tests and requests our transmission of Internet packets to your computer. ShieldsUP!! benignly probes the target computer at your location. Since these probings must travel from **our** server to **your** computer, you should be certain to have administrative right-of-way to conduct protocol tests through any and all equipment located between your computer and the Internet.

NO INFORMATION gained from your use of these services will be retained, viewed or used by us or anyone else in any way for any purpose whatsoever.

If you are using a personal firewall product which LOGS contacts by other systems, you should expect to see entries from this site's probing IP addresses: 4.79.142.192 –thru– 4.79.142.207. Since we own this IP range, these packets will be from us and will NOT BE ANY FORM OF MALICIOIUS INRUSION ATTEMPT OR ATTACK on your computer. You can use the report of their arrival as a handy confirmation that your intrusion logging systems are operating correctly, but please do not be concerned with their appearance in your firewall logs. It's expected.

Proceed

Before clicking on "Proceed" take the time to notice if the following paragraph is shown on your screen. If the screen appears, Gibson Research has already discovered your computer's unique IP address. An "IP address" is comparable to your mailing address. Your IP address is being made known to an Internet site when you log on.

You'll see a screen similar to the one that appears on the following page:

The text below might uniquely

identify you on the Internet

Your Internet connection's IP address is uniquely associated with the following "machine name":

h234.142.133.60.ip.telco.net

The string of text above is known as your Internet connection's "reverse DNS." The end of the string is probably a domain name related to your ISP. This will be common to all customers of this ISP. But the beginning of the string uniquely identifies your Internet connection. The question is: Is the beginning of the string an "account ID" that is uniquely and permanently tied to you, or is it merely related to your current public IP address and thus subject to change?

The concern is that any web site can easily retrieve this unique "machine name" (just as we have) whenever you visit. It may be used to uniquely identify you on the Internet. In that way it's like a "supercookie" over which you have no control. You can not disable, delete, or change it. Due to the rapid erosion of online privacy, and the diminishing respect for the sanctity of the user, we wanted to make you aware of this possibility. Note also that reverse DNS may disclose your geographic location.

If the machine name shown above is only a version of the IP address, then there is less cause for concern because the name will change as, when, and if your Internet IP changes. But if the machine name is a fixed account ID assigned by your ISP, as is often the case, then it will follow you and not change when your IP address does change. It can be used to persistently identify you as long as you use this ISP.

There is no standard governing the format of these machine names, so this is not something we can automatically determine for you. If several of the numbers from your current IP address (**62.133.127.328**) appear in the machine name, then it is likely that the name is only related to the IP address and not to you. But you may wish to make a note of the machine name shown above and check back from time to time to see whether the name follows any changes to your IP address, or whether it, instead, follows you.

Just something to keep in mind as you wander the Internet.

Now, "click" on the "Proceed" button. The entire **Shields UP!!** page of the site is now replaced. Read through it. Notice that "Shields Up Services" horizontal menu bar, which is located on the bottom-half of the page that is being displayed, has the following tests that can be run:

- File Sharing
- Common Ports
- All Service Ports
- Messenger Spam
- Browser Headings

Run each of the **Shields UP** tests on your system. The horizontal menu bar appears at the bottom of each subsequent page. Following is a brief discussion of what you will learn from each test of your system:

What does Running the "File Sharing" Test Determine?

The results of File Sharing will show you whether GRC (Gibson Research) was able to connect to your computer's hidden Internet server. Should that happen anyone on the Internet could turn your computer into his or her personal slave without your knowledge! The bad guys would be able to steal your connection's bandwidth and resources.

The hidden server could be sending your private information out to others or masking the identity of a person who wishes to use your system to commit crimes.

What does Running the "Common Ports" Test Determine?

A certain number of the 65,000+ Internet ports are particularly troublesome. Many of them are associated with standard functions, such as Port 80 that is used for HTTP or web traffic, or Port 21 which is typically used for FTP or File Transfer Protocols. An unsecure and "open" port can be read by any hacker and can provide a direct reference to <u>known</u> vulnerabilities on the hardware and software you are using.

What does Running the "All Services Port" Test Determine?

Running the "All Services Port" test checks your system to determine if any ports are open. This particular scan may take a while. You will also learn whether your computer will respond to a variety of external requests to supply information about your computer's internal secrets.

What does Running the "Messenger Spam" Test Determine?

The "Messenger Spam" test allows you to find out if you can be spammed. Gibson sends a small number of packets to your Internet address. Your computer or Internet service provider (ISP) isn't blocking message traffic if you receive the message.

What does Running the "Browser Header" Test Determine?

You may be passing information to a website that you have visited without your knowledge. The exact information is difficult to determine. You should be very interested in knowing what your Internet browser is sending to the websites you contact.

Hackers are very good at gathering small pieces of information on their targets from various sources and putting together a bigger picture.

Additional information on Internet security is available in the **Shields UP!!** series of tests and services. These additional features allow you to customize requests to gain additional information about specific ports on your computer.

You are encouraged to return to the "Home" page for Gibson Research and read their educational materials and learn more about the software they produce.

Other Tips on How to Plug the Holes

Other vulnerabilities can exist in your computing environment that malicious users, who want to harm your computer or steal information, can exploit. The remainder of this chapter addresses a number of them. You should be able to affirmatively answer each of the following questions:

---

1. Have you recently installed all patches and updates for the software on your computer?

You need to be able to answer "Yes!" to the above question or your system is vulnerable to an attack.

Software publishers send out updates and patches for a reason. They have learned that something is wrong with their software. Try as they may, software publishers have difficulty producing software that is error free. Most software is released with "bugs". Normally, it takes months or years for all of the problems in a particular edition of software to be discovered.

Responsible software publishers regularly offer patches to "plug the holes". The information technology industry fights a constant battle against bugs and security flaws. You are, at the very least, responsible (and in some cases may be legally liable) for downloading and installing software patches and updates.

You are, otherwise, consciously allowing doors to be left open to your system if you fail to regularly update your computer applications.

Your lack of action virtually places your computer on a targeted list for intrusion and might very well be considered a failure to exercise *due diligence* in a court of law. "Downstream liability" for failure to responsibly operate information infrastructure is becoming a legal issue.

---

2. Do you routinely back-up your critical information?

We have become increasingly dependent upon the information stored on our computers. Your checkbook, accounting information, valuable documents, and proprietary information must be protected. You are responsible for taking steps to protect valuable data that you can't afford to lose.

Computers and software will fail. The reason can be mechanical, electronic-related or man-made, but a computer system <u>will</u> fail. The only question is *when*. Important information will be lost if you haven't taken steps to protect it. Computer users should be prepared.

You can back-up your system using commercially published software or do so yourself. You can use compact disks, back-up drives or an on-line storage service. Regardless, you must take action.

---

3. Do you secure your workstation when you walk away?

You need to control access to your computer. People could destroy, damage or contaminate your data on purpose or accidentally. The same thing is true about the computer itself. You need to take proactive measures to protect your information resources.

Lock your computer's keyboard when you walk away from your system. That is one way to keep people from accessing your confidential data. Otherwise, anyone who comes along in your absence can sit down at your unattended computer and begin perusing your data or gaining unauthorized access to your system

---

4. Do you use strong passwords?

You should use strong, robust passwords or passphrases. That is another way to provide extra protection for your system. Skilled intruders can beat simple passwords with what is known as brute force attacks.

Make it a habit to create strong and complex passwords. They represent your first line of security when unauthorized individuals decide to intrude upon your information resources.

If you own a business and have more than a few employees you should consider creating a company-wide password policy and educating employees on how to follow through upon it. The alternative is to risk an unauthorized individual gaining access to your records and confidential information.

A strong password, generally, should be longer in length (i.e. between 8 and 14 characters or more) rather than shorter, contain both upper and lower case alphabetic letters and specialized alphanumeric characters.

An example of such a password would be: SaM#XXxx5%.

A passphrase may also be used. It is more complex than a password and thus provides even better security. A passphrase might also be easier to remember. An example of a "passphrase" that can be easily remembered might be one that includes special characters such as:

$Lillies*Grow*Tall*in*the*Summer$

Regardless of a password or passphrase's strength, you should avoid writing it down or sharing it with others. Avoid using passwords or phrases that have their origin in the popular culture. You should also avoid including personal information in your password (i.e. your birth date or a pet's name). Cyber thieves are clever.

Passwords or passphrases should be changed frequently to remain viable and be unrelated to any previously used passwords. For example, avoid replacing one password such as "Jim's$PassPhrase$" with a new password that is similar such as:

"Jim's%NewPassPhrase%".

Computer users should also avoid using common words, such as vegetables or fruit, as passwords. Malicious users trying to gain access to your information can use easily available hacker tools to conduct what is known as a "dictionary attack". Modern day computers are so fast that they can quickly test every word in the dictionary and identify a simple password.

Consider checking the strength or robustness of your password. Microsoft™ provides a useful on-line password-checking site. Type in the password you propose to test and observe the real-time assessment of the password's strength. The URL is:

https://www.microsoft.com/protect/fraud/passwords/checker.aspx?WT.mc_id= Site_Link

The purpose for using passwords or passphrases is to help assure the confidentially, integrity and availability of information assets. A prudent computer user may want to consider using additional techniques to improve user authentication.

5. Are you filtering the flow of information to and from the Internet?

The Internet is a chaotic and ungoverned environment. You must take steps to block intrusions and filter incoming and outgoing information from your system. Otherwise, your vital information becomes a potential target when you connect to the Internet.

Attacks against your computer can originate from anywhere on the planet. If it is possible for intruders to get inside of your computer system from the Internet they will likely do so. Blocking or controlling Internet access is essential. Installing a personal software and/or a hardware firewall is the next-best alternative to staying off of the Internet in the first place.

We will discuss the topic of firewalls in greater detail in a later section.

6. *Are your hardware and software assets physically safe?*

Is your computer left in a secure condition when you leave your work space? Can a person on the night cleaning crew, for example, simply pick up your computer and walk away with it? Controlling physical access to your vital workspace can eliminate a host of vulnerabilities.

Insiders cause a significant amount of the damage that occurs to an individual's or organization's infrastructure. An unlocked door, for example, makes it possible for a disgruntled employee or visitor to gain proximity to your critical data. Locking the door or turning off your computer would be an effective security measure against individuals wishing to do harm to your information assets. Other methods would include issuing restricted access cards to employees, install hand or finger print readers or other form of biometric authentication (i.e. for definitions see www.computer-security-glossary.org).

7. *Do you encrypt your critical data?*

You should encrypt your critical data. Many people simply fail to do so. Your computer, if stolen, and its contents would be an open book to thieves once they get past your password. If your information is encrypted there is a possibility that confidential information would remain safe.

One major software publisher, Microsoft™, publishes a security website to help users: www.microsoft.com/protect/default.aspx. Included are suggestions on how to secure your home computer and information assets. Microsoft's™ site also contains additional tips and services that would be useful.

Summary

You must protect your information assets from persons who are able to gain unauthorized access. Encryption of confidential data or using an encrypted connection can be a very effective solution.

Chapter 3

Obtain and Use Security Software

You can buy software to help you secure your computer. This class of software is typically referred to as "antivirus" software or "security suites". It provides protection against known viruses as well as Trojan horses, worms and other malware. Some commercially available security software contains additional features, such as being able to work as a personal firewall and other programs that help make your computer more safe.

You should first consider what level of protection you want for your computer. Almost certainly you would decide to buy a product that blocks viruses. The best computer security software maintains and frequently updates a database of known virus signatures.

Antivirus software "scans" the files on your computer for known virus signatures and any other software invaders that need to be identified and removed. Most computer security "suites" also protect your system against a full-range of malware (viruses, Trojan horses, worms, etc.) and a feature that includes an update service that can be downloaded which should last for the duration of the license.

Security experts highly recommend that you install antivirus software on your computer. They also recommend that you enable the software to frequently connect to the software publisher's website and download and install all updates on your computer.

But which product should you use?

The decision is yours. We will examine several major security software publishers who enjoy good reputations. Each company offers a number of products and services. You must discriminate among each in terms of prices, features and service.

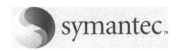

Symantec Corporation sells a number of products. The ones for home use are Norton Antivirus, Internet Security and Norton 360. You can examine the features of each at the following URL: http://us.norton.com/index.jsp

Symantec also publishes a variety of security software for business use. You can access the following site to study the features of each category of Symantec products at the following URL: http://www.symantec.com/business/index.jsp

Another publisher of computer security software is AVG. The AVG website is helpful and explains the features of each product. AVG is marketed in a variety of packages with varying features and prices. You can learn more about the product line at the following URL:

http://www.avg.com/us-en/homepage.

Anyone interested may download a "free trial" offer.

Kaspersky publishes a full line of home and business security products as well as mobile based security solutions. Descriptions of the various products available from Kaspersky may be reviewed at the following URL:

http://usa.kaspersky.com

McAfee

McAfee is a well known publisher of antivirus and security software. McAfee has a product mix that is similar to other publishers. The McAfee website also contains useful information on cyber threats. One product, for example, is designed specifically for home use while another is for businesses. You can access information on McAfee at the following URL:

http://www.mcafee.com/us/.

There are other basic computer security products that can be purchased.

What factors should you consider when purchasing a security software package?

The following features should be considered prior to your settling upon a security software product to purchase:

- Your Needs
- The Price
- Product Features
- Compatibility
- Support
- Licensing

A discussion of each component follows.

a. Your Needs

Determine what you need before you purchase security software. You would want a feature rich computer security software package if you need to protect a small business network with five or more computers. The number of computers you must protect is important.

Do you need mobile protection? Do you need to provide for *intrusion detection*? (See www.computer-security-glossary.org for definitions.)

Determine your specific security needs and then begin your search for the package that has features which address the problem you want to solve.

b. The Price

Rarely do you find antivirus or security software priced below $39.95. Expect to pay at least that much to obtain a basic security product. You might be able to find freeware or shareware products that offer some of the features you need but unless you want to devote a significant amount of time learning and maintaining the software you are better off purchasing one of the better-known products.

c. Product Features

Among desirable features you likely want would be one that blocks all malicious software from the Internet as well as e-mail. That would include viruses, Trojan horses and spyware. You may also want a personal firewall.

You would need the software product you are considering to allow for the automatic and frequent updating of known viruses. Hackers, crackers and cyber criminals are on a continual quest to develop new and better attacks against your computer. New malicious code is being released daily.

Some security software publishers offer additional features in which you might be interested. Included might be the previously mentioned personal firewall, or features that optimize disk storage and utilities that can check for lost documents or files and also check your system for other weaknesses or vulnerabilities. Consider the choices carefully.

d. Compatibility

Make sure that the product you settle upon is compatible with your computer's brand and edition of your operating system. Avoid paying a visit to an on-line auction site and purchasing your antivirus software. You might find that your inexpensive purchase turns out to be a bust due to incompatibility, or worse yet, proves to contain flaws and vulnerabilities.

e. Support

Determine what type of technical support the publisher of the security software you are considering supplies. Most offer on-line FAQ (Frequently Asked Questions) support. A number of software publishers provide live technical telephone support. Some provide live support for free. Others will provide support for a short period of time and thereafter bill you on a per-incident basis.

Call the support number of the publisher you are considering to determine how you are received as a potential customer. Your initial contact is likely to be as good as it gets relative to support.

Make your purchasing decision accordingly.

f. Licensing

Product licensure is likely to be different for many publishers. You want to know what restrictions, if any, are placed on your use of the product. One of the most important issues today is the need to install the same security software on both your desktop and laptop computers.

Most publishers only license their product for one machine or CPU (see www.computer-security-glossary.org for definition). Others may permit something different or offer some type of packaged deal for the desktop, lap-top and mobile devices. Be sure that you understand the licensing requirement of the product you are considering.

Purchase and use basic security software. There really isn't any excuse for failing to do so.

Chapter 4

Get a Firewall and Use It

There are two types of firewalls. One is a software program and the other is a specialized hardware device. Both are designed to prevent unauthorized access to a computer or a network.

The main function of a firewall is to examine the contents of *each* in-bound and out-bound Internet data packet. The messages are either allowed to pass or they are blocked based upon the policies or rules that are established by the computer owner. A firewall monitors and takes note of attempts to move files and data that violate the rules the owner sets.

Firewalls can block communications from specific computers, countries or block information based upon content or services being requested. Firewalls can also block specific computer ports as well. A firewall may be thought of as a "gate keeper" between your computing resources and the Internet. Firewalls, for example, can even prevent an infected computer from "phoning home".

You simply can't afford to allow your computer to connect with every computer that attempts to communicate. Firewalls can give you an opportunity to consider who is attempting to connect with your system and what type of connection is being requested.

Most firewalls maintain a record on what has been sent from the computer and who has attempted to contact your computer. The record is commonly known as "logs". Logs can be studied to obtain additional details.

There are basically two types of firewalls. Software firewalls and hardware firewalls.

1.) Software Firewalls

Security best practices for business and industry include the idea of having and implementing a firewall. Many software publishers offer Internet security software suites that have personal firewall features. Home computers can easily make use of personal software firewalls.

A software firewall provides basic protection against any incoming and outgoing Internet connections. Personal firewalls, as the name implies, resides on an individual's computer. The owner specifies what communication is allowed into or out of the computer (as described at the beginning of this chapter). Personal firewall software also provides for the user to be notified of an attempted breach. A firewall shuts any open doors to your system unless permitted by the owner.

Among the features that should be included with personal firewall software are alerts about in-bound connections. The firewall also informs the user when an application on his or her computer attempts to access the Internet. Firewall software helps to keep your computer from responding to "scans" of your ports.

Software firewalls also can provide information about the individuals, organizations or servers that make illegitimate attempts to connect with your computer. They perform functions that are different from anti-virus software but may be, as mentioned earlier, "packaged" with anti-virus software in suites.

Computer owners, or end-users, implement personal firewalls. Personal firewalls "learn" what connections are authorized by asking the user if an incoming attempt from the Internet is legitimate. Full-featured personal firewall software contains packet filtering (a detail examination of the data contained in Internet packets). Packet filtering monitors and controls how applications on your computer can contact the Internet and more.

Personal firewall products should provide assistance in blocking pop-up ads and cookies. Firewalls should be easy to use for novices and be compatible with different editions of operating system software. A firewall software product should make your system invisible to those who wish to invade it and perform its functions without hampering the other applications on your computer.

Make sure to ask the publisher if the product you are considering is known to have any conflicts with other programs that are typically on personal computers. Call the number that is offered for support and identify yourself as a potential customer. Gauge which product to purchase based upon the product's features, price and quality of pre-sale support.

There are many third-party software firewalls on the market. One website that does a good job of covering personal firewall products and other home security products can be found at: www.firewallguide.com. Among the products that are mentioned are ZoneAlarm and Lavasoft's Personal Firewall.

A number of software firewalls are briefly discussed below:

ZONEALARM by **Check Point**
SOFTWARE TECHNOLOGIES LTD.

ZoneAlarm is a software firewall brand-name published by Check Point (http://www.zonealarm.com/security/en-us/home.htm). The ZoneAlarm firewalls establish security "zones". The Internet is considered to be an *untrusted* zone. ZoneAlarm is available in four different versions: Zone Alarm Pro, Zone Alarm Antivirus, ZoneAlarm Internet Security Suites and ZoneAlarm Extreme. Detailed information is available about the products on the company's website.

COMODO
Creating Trust Online®

Comodo Personal Firewall (www.personalfirewall.comodo.com) has received high reviews. Included in Comodo's features is a component requiring that any software installed on a computer be properly authenticated and monitored. The software is compatible with the most popular operating system and offers an automatic update feature. Users can also upgrade to the paid version of the software which contains more advanced features.

2.) Hardware Firewalls

Firewall hardware, as the name implies, is computer equipment that is placed between your computer and the Internet. Connections are plugged into the firewall device that receives input and output. The basic job that a hardware firewall performs is essentially the same as the software firewall; however, it may possess more robust features, including the capacity to protect more than one computer.

Hardware firewalls, in reality, are telecommunication devices. Like most computer hardware, firewall capabilities have evolved quickly and are likely to be an individual piece of equipment or a component of another hardware device.

The hardware firewall is typically used by businesses and can be customized by setting what is known as security policies. Deploying a hardware firewall is more difficult to set-up and use than a software firewall. Hardware firewalls can be more expensive than a software solution. You can learn more by searching on the Web.

Chapter 5
Put It All Together

Securing your home computer network or business computer network makes common sense and can help you avoid the loss of valuable information or financial resources. An intruder can do more than simply steal your information. The confidential information that you lose might be used to harm others and could make you liable for damages. This can be particularly harmful if you haven't done your due diligence when initially securing your information assets.

STEP 1 - Install Anti-Virus Software

A typical threat faced by a home or small office computer is that of an attack using a virus or malicious software. Webopedia (www.webopedia.com) defines a virus as "a program or piece of code that is loaded onto your computer without your knowledge and runs against your wishes." The malware, in effect, steals your computer's resources and alters its legitimate function.

A virus makes copies of itself. A successful attack can alter the confidentiality, availability or integrity of your computing resources, erase important files or do other serious damage, such as destroying information on your hard drive. A virus can be sent to all of your family members or to the computers of people on your email list.

A virus changes how your computer operates.

You can receive a virus from another program that is passed to you or you can pass along a virus to someone else without your knowledge by sending an infected file. E-mail attachments are among the most popular ways of passing viruses to unsuspecting users.

A virus can virtually be embedded in any file, such as a picture or graphic, e-mail attachment, letter or other document.

Some viruses are capable of running what is known as "executable code". That means a malicious attacker can become aware of everything on your computer, gain access and control your computing resources.

A virus is typically the most common type of malicious code that attacks and infects home office computers. Therefore, you must mitigate the threats by taking appropriate action.

Obtain, install and maintain an anti-virus software package that compares the content of files coming into your computer with a "virus signature database".

Viruses are becoming more sophisticated and powerful. They are being written so they can adapt when they replicate and change or "morph" their basic characteristics or "signatures".

Avoid making the assumption that antivirus software you just bought is the latest version. <u>Changes can occur daily</u>. Remember to routinely visit the publisher's website and download the most recent version of what is known as virus signatures.

There are many different types of malicious software. Among them are worms, Trojan horses and logic bombs. Many security suites address each.

Malicious software differs from "pure" viruses by the way in which they are transported from one user to the next, as well as in the damage that they can do. You must study which security software provides protection from specific threats. You can and should investigate product features.

STEP 2 - Scan and Probe Your Own Computer

You automatically enter a "free-fire zone" when you log-on to the Internet. Your computer is at risk by multiple threats that seek to gain unauthorized access.

Hackers have tools that are freely available on the Internet. These tools can rapidly scan thousands of computers at once to determine which computers are vulnerable. The Internet is loaded with websites from which scanning tools can be downloaded.

Very little technical skill is needed to successfully probe a computer for weaknesses and, if they exist, the hacker can take over a computer and command it to do what he or she wishes.

One thing a hacker might do is inventory the software on your computer, check for known weaknesses and report the results back to the intruder. You might be using a database program, for example, with a known flaw that allows access to your customer records.

The invader could wreak havoc on your computer system. All of your sensitive information would be at risk.

You are unable to stop someone from conducting a scan of the ports on your computer while you are on the Internet. Port scanning isn't against the law, but you do have options.

Use a program or website service to scan or conduct a "white hat hack" on your own computer.

Conduct a "white hat hack" on your system. That would help you discover vulnerabilities and eliminate them. You would then be able to stop your computer from responding to an intruder. The lesson is to become aware of your system's weaknesses and plug the holes before nefarious users discover them.

To repeat, scan your system and eliminate any "holes" or vulnerabilities that are discovered. Do what is necessary to hide your system from hackers.

STEP 3 – Routinely Download and Install Software Updates and Patches

Responsible software publishers have difficulty producing applications that are error free. Most software is released long before all of its flaws or "bugs" are known and understood. Vulnerabilities, as already mentioned, are discovered by the bad guys and exploited.

The worst-case scenario with "buggy" software is that hackers discover the weakness first, then publish them on the Internet. Anyone wishing to use the vulnerability can scan and probe someone's computer to see if the weak point exists, and if it does, ithe malicious hackers can intrude upon your confidential assets.

Software publishers, in all fairness, do try to keep abreast with any flaws and publish what is known as "patches" or "updates" for their individual products. Usually the software fixes can be downloaded free from the publisher's website and installed on your computer.

Entire websites, also, are run by independent businesses that are devoted to maintaining the latest "fixes" and "patches" for the world of computer software.

What type of software packages should you routinely update?

There are basically two types of software. One is operating system software. Operating system software includes Windows 7, Windows Vista, Windows XP,

Windows Server 2003 and Server 2008, any Unix variant, and the Apple OS, etc. Each copy of operating system software that is installed on a computer has a version number. Check the version number of the operating system software you are using to determine whether you need to install updates.

For example, if you have version 3.1 of a particular software package and know patches have been issued for version 3.2 – upgrade your software **IMMEDIATELY**. You can be nearly certain that a vulnerability was discovered in version 3.1.

<u>Application software</u> is the second type of software you should routinely update. Microsoft Office is an example of application software. Depending upon the version number of the application software installed on your computer, you may be vulnerable.

Access the publisher's website. Check to see if you have the latest software updates installed. Download the latest patches and updates and install them if you have a previous version.

The computer owner has the responsibility to routinely check to make sure all of the "holes" in his or her computer system software are closed. The patches, fixes or upgrades must be regularly updated as part of a security plan to protect your information resources.

 STEP 4 - Install a Firewall

You may recall in an earlier chapter we recommended that either a software or hardware firewall should be installed to prevent unauthorized access to a computer or a network.

Firewalls examine the content of each message that tries to enter or leave your computer. A firewall either accepts or blocks the movement of files and documents based upon the rules or policies that you, the owner, define.

Firewalls can block communications from specific computers or block information based upon content. Firewalls can also block specific ports or services.

You simply can't afford to accept a connection with every computer that wishes to communicate with you. You need to give yourself an opportunity to study what type of connection is being attempted with your computer and know why an outside computer is trying to make contact with you.

Most firewalls maintain a log file on what has been sent to your computer and from your computer and by whom. The log file can be thought of as a "paper trail". Logs can be studied to obtain additional details on all outgoing and incoming messages.

 STEP 5 - Use Robust Passwords

A <u>password</u> is a set of text or special characters that makes it possible for a user to control access to his or her program, document, file or network.

Home and small business computer users should routinely use passwords. Passwords should even be used to re-authenticate when you have ended a work session and return.

An individual's password(s) should be unique and easy to remember for the user. A robust password should be established because brute force attacks can break a password.

A strong password should contain a combination of upper and lower case letters and possibly contain special characters, also.

Avoid writing your password or passwords down on paper. Make sure that when you enter the password to gain access to your computer you don't allow someone to observe you and steal the password.

Passwords should also be changed frequently.

STEP 6 - Terminate Your Internet Connection and Turn off Your Computer

People frequently leave their computers on and connected to a persistent Internet connection when they walk away from their work stations, leave for the day or go to bed at night. Maintaining an always "on" Internet connection is dangerous and should be avoided.

A good security practice is to either lock your keyboard or terminate your Internet connection when you leave your computer or workstation. Better yet, turn off the Internet connection when you have retrieved the information you need.

Maintaining an open-connection has several disadvantages. First, you are open to active scanning. Second, anyone who gains access to your unprotected computer can use it. Third, certain editions of software become unstable the longer that a computer remains "on".

Your computer, while it is operating, creates a large number of temporary files. Those files remain in memory if the user fails to turn the computer off or simply leaves the computer powered up and connected to the Internet.

The bottom line is that the integrity of your computer system may be successfully compromised if you don't terminate the Internet and turn off your machine. Your computer is a sitting target when it is connected to the Internet.

When you terminate your Internet connection or turn off a computer system, your computer denies access to anyone who tries to gain entrance to your computer.

 STEP 7 - Beware of E-mail Attachments

E-mail was one of the first applications developed for use on the Internet.

E-mail made it possible to transmit text messages and files over the Internet. Most e-mails consist of text; however, some e-mails contain "attachments". An attachment can be a graphic, a sound file, or any other type of file or document.

Typically, e-mail programs have a text-editor associated with them which is like a word processor. You can create, store, print-out and forward e-mail. E-mail is extremely fast and travels over the Internet from the sender to the receiver quickly. E-mail is harmless by itself.

Most computers and networks are set up to receive e-mail.

You might well imagine, though, that since most computers are configured to receive e-mail that <u>attachments to e-mail are a common method used to transmit computer viruses and exploit weaknesses</u>.

Most people with access to the Internet receive far more e-mail than they choose. An entire class of e-mail known as "spam" (similar to unwanted telemarketing calls) floods the in-boxes of computer users.

Before you open up an e-mail or an attachment, make sure you know who the sender is. Ask yourself the following questions: "Am I expecting this information?" "Do I know the sender?" "Is there a possibility the attachment could be dangerous?"

If the answer is "yes" to the last question, scan the attachment for a virus or avoid opening it all together. Delete the entire message if there is any reason to question the email's origin or purpose.

You should make sure that your anti-virus program is set up to scan each incoming e-mail for known viruses or malicious code.

 STEP 8 - Establish a Disaster Recovery Plan

You are very likely to lose critical data at some point in time.

You need to accept the fact that it's only a question of <u>when</u> you are going to lose important data not <u>if</u> you are going to lose vital information.

Loss of data can occur as a result of an intentional act or security breach, an accident, a hardware or software failure or an Act of God. The important thing to remember is that a loss of your critical data **WILL** occur.

Part of a strong information security plan is to take the necessary steps to ensure that you have a copy of your critical information and can restore it. Having a plan to restore is known as "disaster recovery".

Creating a complete and viable back-up of your critical data isn't casual or accidental. Systematically backing up your data is a business process. It requires thorough planning and practice. Your disaster recovery program should operate from the following mind-set: everything should be done to assure the integrity of your personal information and/or the operation of your business without significant cost or inconvenience.

A back-up of your information requires both hardware and software. When there is a loss of data, the back-up file should be capable of "restoring" the original information sets. Restoring of backed up data for your home or small business computer is essential.

An effective backup plan requires conducting regular disaster recovery activities, such as making a separate copy of important files and storing it in a different location. Your critical data should be backed up at least once a week or daily, if necessary

 STEP 9 - Use Encryption

Data can be hidden so that if someone happens to obtain sensitive information it would be impossible to be read. When a computer user turns a readable file or document into one that is unreadable it is said that the data has been "encrypted". Data encryption makes it easier to maintain the confidentiality of information.

Encrypted files require that they be opened with a "key" in order to be read. A key is a shared secret between the sender and receiver.

Many software applications come with an option to encrypt data. Otherwise, you can purchase encryption software or visit a shareware site and download a free or trial version of a commercial product.

Encrypting data may seem like an extreme step; however, people who want access to steal your computing resources are becoming more numerous. Attack methods are more sophisticated and stealing information pays off.

Law enforcement is rarely able to recover any losses that you incur as a result of cyber theft.

A Final Word

We live and operate in what is known as an *asymmetric threat environment*. We must develop a new awareness of national, commercial and personal security. Much of the threat comes from the Internet. Attacks against your computing resources can and will arrive at your "door step" from any number of sources.

The variety of the threats arrayed against our digital processing infrastructure (computers and networks) comes from organized crime, hackers, script kiddies, cyber espionage and terrorism.

You must carefully conduct business and your personal affairs on the computer and take extraordinary steps to protect your information assets. Your essential information is a target in an on-going global information war.

You are protecting your personal assets and maintaining a competitive advantage when you shield your information assets. Choosing to do otherwise will place your business and livelihood at risk.

Additional Security Tips

1. Consider disabling scripting languages (i.e. Java, Java Scripts and Active X) in your browser.

2. Disable hidden file extensions (such as .exe and .vbs).

3. Avoid downloading and installing add-on tool bars, screen-savers, etc.

4. Avoid downloading and running programs from an unknown source.

5. Make a boot disk to help recover from a system crash.

6. Adjust browser settings to the highest possible level.

7. Be certain that you have hidden the SSID if using a wireless router.

8. Turn off the pre-viewing pane in your e-mail program.

9. Avoid surfing on "fringe" websites that deal in questionable content.

10. Avoid clicking on "OK" with pop-up ads.

11. Avoid clicking on e-mail hyperlinks.

12. Only install legitimate and properly licensed copies of software.

13. Answer "No" when asked by website, "Remember My Password?"

14. Encrypt data that is going to be used on a wireless network.

15. Make sure that when you are using WPA 2 security with your wireless networks, the feature is turned-on.

16. Routinely run software maintenance utilities, such as disk defragmenter and check disk.

17. Avoid sharing files directly with an unfamiliar computer, such as plugging-in a USB drive into another computer or vice-versa.

18. Become familiar with the security provisions of your favorite social media site. Use the highest level of security settings available.

19. Change the default settings (i.e. name and pre-set password) associated with your wireless router and any other hardware that you use.

20. Use multi-factored authentication when you can.

21. Hover over any suspicious link you might receive. Look in the status line to determine if the URL is legitimate.

22. Make sure that you are on a secure site (https:) when shopping online.

23. Consider installing a remote access location tool on your lap top, iPad or smart phone. You would be able to wipe confidential records clean.

24. Download only from trusted sites.

25. Make multiple back-ups of your critical data.

26. Use an external hard disk drive with your computer.

27. Maintain ALL of your software's installation disks.

28. Disable all unused programs on your system.

29. Consider disabling all use of Java, Javascript and Active X. Realize your interaction with favorite websites might change.

30. Consider using a browser password.

31. Make a record of the serial numbers inscribed on your hardware devices. Take a picture of each device.

32. Disable print and file shares on your system if you can do so without disrupting the use of a printer on your home network.

33. Consider changing any default settings on software that you use.

34. Consider using anti-key logger software.

35. Avoid using public computers (i.e. business centers, cyber cafe's, etc.).

36. Encrypt all hard drives, USB drives or any other external storage media.

37. Consider purchasing a VPN or Virtual Private Network from a provider.

38. Become aware of the security challenges emerging with embedded computers.

39. Disable "cookies"; however, you can expect difficulty with accessing some of your favorite websites.

Visit www.computer-security-glossary.org for more information.

www.ingramcontent.com/pod-product-compliance
Lightning Source LLC
Chambersburg PA
CBHW082114070326
40689CB00052B/4672